SWAMP CANDLES

BY JACK BARRY

Wh[illegible] happen old English Majors?
Jack

Down-to-Earth Books
Ashfield, Massachusetts

SWAMP CANDLES

By Jack Barry

Down-to-Earth Books

P. O. Box 488

Ashfield, Massachusetts

413-628-0227

March, 2006

ISBN: 1-878115-22-7

Dedication

For Rochelle

Introduction

What, **more** haiku? You might think that a world staggering under its own weight couldn't bear even one more 'slim volume.' Maybe it's because I'm left-handed, but I think that efforts such as these—solitary, slow, unpaid and barely noticed—can do more to lift to the world than drag it down.

Here is where I could hold forth on the necessity of honest literature, how humans need language to make meaning, how a culture as venerable as the Australian Aborigines actually sang their world into its very existence! If that seemed too far fetched I'd point out that to this day all we 'modern people' are still dead dependent on words, which flesh out what would otherwise be a world of shadowy feelings and unnamed objects.

But this is just a little book of haiku. Haiku, of course, is the atom of the literary world, the smallest form that can stand on its own. Not only does that make it handy to write, it also makes it ideally suited for helping **notice** this blooming, buzzing confusion; haiku is for saying what **is**, before that moment disappears as if it had never occurred. So a book like this is a record of otherwise lost moments, and every lost moment, every fleeting interaction that disappears without notice renders our world that much less interesting, that much less vital, that much closer to being trampled by feet that aren't watching. It is to this steady trampling—the ignorance, indifference, the scorn for life that is barbarism—that I address this book, enlisting the quiet power of haiku to help save our lovely little blue and green planet.

Of course, that's a lot to ask from such little poems. But I once read a book by Thor Heyerdahl about his expedition to Easter Island. Being a practical man, Mr. Heyerdahl was stumped by all those statues, some of which are forty feet tall and weigh up to fifty tons, dragged for miles and erected by people who'd never even heard of a horse. After much prodding he got a few of the older islanders to hint that they might know the secret, and one sunny South Pacific day they set out to show him what they knew. In full view of the modern, color-photographed world, those Easter Islanders managed to raise one of the fallen statues, using no more than a couple of long poles and bushels of little stones.

It was the little stones that got my interest. Using the poles as levers, the old men pried the block until it jerked high enough to admit one small stone. Then they heaved some more, squeezing a second stone beside the first, continuing the process for days, weeks, one small stone on top of the other until, at last, that long-fallen statue stood again.

The weight of human indifference is just as heavy as those forbidding faces. I feel it every time I squeeze into the morning traffic, hear the blaring radio, read the blaring paper. And yes, saving a planet's a lot to ask from a few tiny poems. But what do we have, if we don't have poetry? So please sit back, make yourself comfortable, while I take aim and toss out my first handful of little stones...

November '05

1.

New Year's morning
starting the fire
with last night's coals

wing feathers
etched in fresh snow
the bare blue sky

snow at dusk
the bony mare
lifts her one white foot

frost in the windows
the crescent moon's
two sharp points

a single deer's track
finally leads into
the black stream

almost dark
blinking snowflakes
i can't see

ten below zero
empty gloves
reach for the fire

snow storm rages
deeper and deeper
inside

long after it fell
snow still pulling down
silence

shadows deepen
fresh coyote tracks
the rising moon

warm spot
where the cat was sleeping
full moon on snow

my breath
on cold glass
watching for you

2.

warm cat
sniffs the cold cat
coming in

the moon through black trees
one distant owl
answers another

night funeral
a bare branch's
quivering shadow

frozen trees
pop all night
the silent stars

fallen asleep
the needle still glinting
in the quilter's hand

moon
just after full
the color of old snow

half way through winter
both halves of a butternut shell
chewed through

new kids next door
roll the same
old snowman

dangling from
the broken water pump
a perfect icicle

ice-bowed hemlocks
i lean closer
to the page

barbed wire
grown into old pines
winter rain

rain on the roof
your hand squeezes mine
as i pull up your blankets

3.

snow into mud
the pale horse
stands on three legs

black pond
swallowing snow flakes
a goose bends to drink

still more snow
the pregnant ewe's
muddy knees

calling for a lost dog
the wind cuts through
the hole in my coat

blue snow shadows
the farmer’s hand pulls
the barn door shut

perched on
the one dry step
March sun

two red winged blackbirds
waiting for the snow to melt
two hundred crows

Spring Equinox
where the wood pile stood
a hole in the snow

sparrows steal threads
from the scarecrow's tattered shirt
the last of the snow

dead branch
finally falling
spring rain

canoe stuck
in the mud again
following clouds

woken by the wind
the rise and fall
of your soft breath

4.

full cemetery
the young widow points out
the first snow drops

April ice
barely holds
my thin shadow

bare branches
bent with swallows
patter of rain

brown grass
still holds the shape
of last winter's snow

new mare next door
the gelding stares over
a single electric wire

orphaned lamb
calls after the others
the rushing wind

midnight church bells
two geese glide around
the last sliver of moon

bending her cane
to straighten
drooping daffodils

dragging her jacket
home from school
first spring peepers

one arm
out of the blankets
April sunrise

melting frost
a wasp taps against
the sun-warmed window

she brings me cake
i bring her
the empty tins

5.

looking up the name
of the wildflower
i just trampled

neighbors squat
on front porch steps
a chorus of peepers

turning the garden
the wire fence
hums in the wind

planting gladiolus
dirt on the bottom
of her white feet

the mother alone
as the school bus drives away
falling apple blossoms

at first
not feeling
drizzle

cold rain
soft taps inside
the last goose egg

picking dandelions
the neighbor's girl waves
at passing cars

watching the frog
kick deeper into the pond
the cool in my palm

before I can turn
kingfisher
far from its splash

rustle of marsh grass
a dragonfly inches out of
its graying husk

pulling me closer
under the blankets
songbirds at dawn

6.

lilacs in bloom
a swallowtail crosses
the double yellow line

first two bean leaves
open to the sun
a cat bird's cry

a baby's voice
in the other room
dawn through the curtains

neighborhood children
follow the road crew
wind-tossed daisies

solstice sunrise
a startled fox
disappears

sun straight up
half way out of the sink
the spider slips again

longest day
the slowest duckling
tries to catch up

lost kite
rising in a cloudless sky
a child’s cry

shelling snap peas
the eldest sister’s
swollen fingers

drying blood
of the dead fox kit
traffic flowing by

silence after thunder
a damselfly's
shaking wings

raindrops knock off
mountain laurel blossoms
waiting for you

7.

heat wave
a hornet nest balloons
in the woodpile

eyeballing sunrise
the bull frog's
bulging throat

noon heat
the next log whines
through the saw blade

napping baby's
sweaty upper lips
bees in the azaleas

the dog's tongue
bicycles lie flat
under the big maple

heat of the day
moving the argument
to the shade

red sunset
the hermit thrush reaches
a higher note

a white pigeon wheels
into the open hayloft
mid-summer dusk

first evening cool
a preening goose
stretches one wing

between roars
of the bullfrogs
the ticking clock

yellow moon
soaked in fog
the last swamp candles

thunder passes
without rain
waiting for you

8.

noon heat
a big ant struggles
through wet paint

a cicada’s rattle
slowly unwinds
still no rain

pasture turning brown
the foal stays close
behind his mother

red sunrise
the great blue heron's
muddy knees

thunderheads
crowd the tree line
the heron leans lower

the beaver's wake
touches both shores
first drops of rain

counting the seconds
between lightning and thunder
rain tapping leaves

releasing a tattered moth
back into the night
last quarter moon

late summer wind
covering one bare foot
with the other

morning fog
not letting the screen door
slam

skipping stones
speaking of people
no longer here

cut hay
lies in the rain
waiting for you

9.

vanished before
my breath on the glass
three deer at dawn

starlings strung
along a wire
dripping fog

falling leaves
small faces peer from
a yellow school bus

bumblebees inside
each beach rose
church bells from town

first cricket
in a brown field
a crow hops twice

caught in the orchard
at dawn
the fawn’s fading spots

second day of school
another ripe pear
thumps out back

home after
looking for the lost cat
a handful of wildflowers

a red tailed hawk
cries on the wind
pulling rusty nails

mist over cut hay
a barn cat rubs
the farmer's stubbled chin

reaching deeper
into the beach plums
a herring gull's cry

no answer
to your doorbell
the dripping roof

10.

clear stream
still smoothing
round stones

drifting leaves
cedar waxwings circle back
to the same branch

lifting a bushel
of Empire apples
the farmer's bowed legs

full moon at dawn
the empty logging truck's
clanging chains

frosted goldenrod
a dead honey bee's
folded wings

falling children
the backyard fills
with yellow leaves

blowing on my fingers
halfway home
a field of unpicked pumpkins

frost in the shadows
the great blue heron's
hunched shoulders

a curl of woodsmoke
circles the moon
an owl's silent wings

one goose calls overhead
dark enough to see
the neighbor's lights

rainy Halloween
a hole in the little ghost's
thin sheet

after you go
sunset fills
your empty chair

11.

rain darkens stacked logs
the work horses'
steaming backs

wind through barbed wire
a mourning dove turns
and calls again

home after dark
rose thorns scratch
closed windows

freezing rain
maiden hair fern
gone white

yellow traffic light
blinks to itself
November dusk

stone fire pit
red pine needles bury
the last charred log

neighbor's trash cans
blossom
November rain

a stranger's glance
wet snow slides off
a high slate roof

two men in a ditch
lying about love
rust on their shovels

no mail
turning the umbrella around
on the way back in

before pulling his curtain
my old neighbor
takes a last look

second woodpile
leans against the first
watching for you

12.

black pond
frozen over
the heron circles twice

still no snow
the crumbling banks
of an open grave

snow clouds
the shadows between
the horse's ribs

finding again
the overgrown trail
a dusting of snow

blinking snow
the horse's breath carries
over the fence

black branches
the doe's hoof prints
fill with mud

sleet rattles
brown leaves
a hunter's distant shots

dusk on the shortest day
snow falling
over snow

until
someone told you
sewing in the dark

longest night
the cat snores into
her own fur

split halves of the same log
roll together
in the fire

looking back
after crossing
thin ice